Original title:
The Heart's Voice

Copyright © 2024 Swan Charm
All rights reserved.

Author: Liina Liblikas
ISBN HARDBACK: 978-9916-89-646-4
ISBN PAPERBACK: 978-9916-89-647-1
ISBN EBOOK: 978-9916-89-648-8

Murmurs of the Soul

Soft whispers in the night,
Secrets dance in shadowed light.
Gentle breezes carry dreams,
Silver moondust gently gleams.

Echoes of a heart once soared,
Wings of hope, a tale explored.
In stillness, truths begin to weave,
In every breath, the soul believes.

Lyrics of the Untold

Verses penned in silent ink,
Words unspoken make us think.
Hidden depths beneath our skin,
Stories wait for light to win.

In the shadows, voices call,
Truths arise, and fears may fall.
Listen close, the whispers play,
A symphony in night and day.

Sonnet of the Organs

Heartbeats thrum in rhythmic bliss,
A love song wrapped in every kiss.
Lungs draw in the fragrant air,
Life pulses with a beating flair.

Fingers dance on strings of fate,
Each note played, a bond innate.
In the silence, organs sigh,
Melodies of life go by.

Rhapsody of Longing

In the distance, shadows sigh,
Underneath a twilight sky.
Yearning hearts in soft refrain,
Chasing echoes of sweet pain.

Waves of time roll in and out,
Nights of longing, dreams devout.
In the silence, hope remains,
Whispers of love break the chains.

Vibrations of Longing

In the stillness of night,
Whispers call to the stars,
Echoes of a heartbeat,
Longing stretches afar.

Soft winds carry hopes,
Through the shadows they weave,
Yearning deep as the sea,
In silence, we believe.

Every glance that we share,
Sparks a flame in the dark,
Flickers of distant dreams,
A symphony, a spark.

Time stands still in the hush,
Moments linger, then fade,
Yet within the silence,
Our longing is displayed.

In the dance of the moon,
Desires find their own voice,
Amidst the quiet night,
Longing makes us rejoice.

Melodies of Affection

In gentle notes we find,
The warmth of your embrace,
Every chord a reminder,
Of love's sweet, tender grace.

Laughter rings in the air,
Like a songbird's first flight,
Melodies of affection,
Make the world feel so bright.

With every soft whisper,
A tune plays in the heart,
Binding souls together,
Never shall we part.

In the rhythm of closeness,
Two hearts beat as one sound,
An orchestra of feelings,
In love's harmony, we're bound.

Through the seasons we share,
Our song will always rise,
Melodies of affection,
Written 'neath endless skies.

Resonance of Dreams

In the dawn's early light,
Dreams start to take their flight,
Visions dance through the air,
Filling hearts with delight.

Whispers of possibilities,
Call to the brave and bold,
Every heartbeat a promise,
Every dream to behold.

In the tapestry woven,
Stars twinkle in the night,
Resonance of our hopes,
Guides us with its light.

Through valleys of shadows,
Visions shimmer and beam,
With courage we embrace,
The beauty of our dream.

As the night fades away,
And dawn breaks anew,
We chase the resonance,
Of dreams that feel so true.

Palette of Passion

In colors so vivid,
Hearts paint love's sweet embrace,
Every stroke tells a story,
Every hue a warm trace.

From crimson to amber,
Bright flames of desire,
Each brush of your fingers,
Sets my soul on fire.

With lavender whispers,
And shades of soft blue,
The palette of passion,
Is crafted just for you.

Golden rays of the sun,
Outline our sacred dance,
In every burst of color,
Lives our bold romance.

As night falls with a hush,
Stars dot the canvas high,
Our love is the artwork,
That will never say goodbye.

Duet of Desire

In shadows soft, where whispers sigh,
Hearts entwined beneath the sky.
A dance of dreams, a fleeting glance,
Two souls ignited in a trance.

The night unveils what words conceal,
With every touch, sensations feel.
A melody of breaths entwined,
In silence, secrets are defined.

Through tangled paths of fate we roam,
In yearning's arms, we find our home.
Together, chasing moonlit streams,
Awakening the deepest dreams.

With every smile, a spark ignites,
A symphony of pure delights.
In tender moments, we confide,
A duet crafted side by side.

As dawn approaches, colors rise,
Reflecting love in morning skies.
In shared embrace, we catch the light,
A duet played in love's pure sight.

Tapestry of Intuition

Threads of thought weave through the air,
A pattern guides with gentle care.
In quiet moments, truths unfold,
A tapestry of dreams retold.

Each color speaks without a voice,
In harmony, we make our choice.
The fabric stretches, bends, and flows,
In serendipity, our essence glows.

Each knot a lesson, tightly bound,
In silent wisdom, we have found.
The weaver's hand, a guiding force,
Through winding paths, we chart our course.

In every stitch, the heart's intent,
A language formed, the soul's ascent.
As time unravels, we embrace,
The threads of life that interlace.

The tapestry, a grand design,
In every hue, your spirit shines.
Together, stitching heart to heart,
In unity, we craft the art.

Pulse of the Unexpressed

Beneath the surface, feelings stir,
A heartbeat whispers, soft and blur.
In shadows deep, unspoken dreams,
The silent language pulls at seams.

In crowded rooms, I feel your shape,
The pulse of time, the breath of fate.
An unseen thread, a gentle tug,
In every glance, the world is drugged.

A canvas waits for colors bold,
The layers hide what can't be told.
In every pause, a message clear,
The rhythm hums, we draw near.

With every sigh, horizons dim,
The unexpressed becomes a hymn.
Each longing glance, a bridge we make,
In silence, love, the risks we take.

And as we dance in shadows' grace,
The pulse ignites, we find our place.
In quiet depths, we merge as one,
The unexpressed, forever spun.

Reflections of the Unsung

In corners dim, where stories lie,
The unsung heroes silently sigh.
With every scar, a tale unfolds,
In whispered breaths, their courage holds.

A light that fades, yet brightly glows,
In shadows cast, their legacy flows.
Each quiet act, a heart's refrain,
The strength in silence, marked by pain.

In fleeting moments, beauty hides,
The unsung notes, the heart abides.
Through trials faced and battles won,
Their spirits rise with setting sun.

In every tear, a truth is found,
Resilient hearts, forever crowned.
Embracing flaws, their light will sing,
As reflections bloom, their praises ring.

So let us honor those who stand,
In whispers soft, they guide our hand.
For in the unsung, stories breathe,
A tapestry of hope we weave.

Breath of the Infinite

In the stillness, time flows slow,
Moments linger, ebb and glow.
Stars whisper secrets in the night,
A canvas painted with pure light.

Infinite dreams in the skies,
Carried softly on moonlit sighs.
Every heartbeat, a timeless dance,
Life unfolds in a cosmic trance.

Waves of endless thoughts collide,
On the shores where hopes abide.
Gentle breezes, a soothing balm,
Nature's pulse, forever calm.

Touch the sky, feel the grace,
Each breath a moment to embrace.
In the silence, worlds unite,
The breath of life, pure and bright.

Together we roam, hand in hand,
In this vast and wondrous land.
Infinite stories, yet untold,
In the heart of the brave and bold.

Whispers of the Soul

In the quiet, secrets dwell,
Softly singing, a gentle bell.
Voices linger, faint and clear,
A melody that draws us near.

With every sigh, a story spun,
Underneath the warming sun.
Echoes dance in twilight's haze,
Crafting dreams in golden rays.

The heart speaks in silent tones,
A language known to all alone.
Through shadows deep, we find the light,
Guided gently into the night.

Tangled paths of fate we weave,
In whispered hopes, we dare believe.
A journey shared, our spirits meet,
In the rhythm of life's heartbeat.

Together we rise, together we fall,
In the silence, we hear it all.
Embracing whispers, both shy and bold,
The whispers of our souls unfold.

Echoes in Silence

Soft voices drift on the breeze,
Carried lightly through the trees.
In the quiet, stories bloom,
Beneath the stars' eternal gloom.

Like shadows dancing in the night,
Echoes fade in soft twilight.
Memories linger, faint and true,
In the hush, they whisper to you.

With every sigh, we reach for more,
An open heart, a silent door.
Words unspoken fill the air,
In the calm, we find the rare.

Time stands still in this sacred space,
An embrace wrapped in quiet grace.
Each heartbeat is a soft refrain,
Echoing wisdom through the pain.

Together we listen, hand in hand,
Riding waves in a timeless land.
In echoes, we find our way,
Guided gently by the day.

Chords of Emotion

Strings of feeling, taut and bright,
Weaving through the day and night.
In each note, a story swells,
A symphony where each heart dwells.

Rhythms pulse like breath in air,
Crafting dreams beyond compare.
Every heartbeat, a gentle tease,
Life's sweet song, a dance with ease.

Through laughter's echoes, tears align,
A tapestry where fates entwine.
In every chord, we find a way,
To bridge the gap of night and day.

Melodies rise, then softly fall,
In each moment, the sweetest call.
Together we play, both near and far,
Guided by love, our shining star.

In the music, hearts ignite,
Chasing shadows into light.
With every song, emotions flow,
In the chords of life, we grow.

Cadence of the Heartstrings

In the hush of twilight's grace,
Gentle whispers find their place.
Softly strumming, beats align,
Melodies of love entwine.

Through the silence, shadows weave,
Hope is born in hearts that cleave.
Every note a dream's embrace,
Echoes linger, time can't chase.

The rhythm sways, a tender dance,
In their gaze, a fleeting chance.
Fingers brush, emotions soar,
In this moment, hearts explore.

Underneath the starlit skies,
Embers glow within your eyes.
Cadence calls, it pulls us near,
Harmony we hold so dear.

As the moonlight softly fades,
In these chords, our truth cascades.
Life's orchestra plays on and on,
Together, we will carry on.

Echoing Truths

In the depths of silence found,
Whispers rise without a sound.
Truths that shimmer, gleam so bright,
Shadows dance in fading light.

Every word a sacred thread,
Woven tales of love widespread.
Across the ages, they resound,
Echoes of the heart profound.

In the chaos, still we seek,
Fragments of the strong and weak.
Voices rise, they intertwine,
Guiding us to what is divine.

Beneath the weight of hidden fears,
Sings the heart through joy and tears.
Ever searching for the key,
In the chaos, we find harmony.

As the sun begins to set,
Echoes linger, we won't forget.
In our souls, the truths we keep,
Love's reflection, vast and deep.

Winds of Intention

Through the trees, the whispers flow,
Carried by the winds that know.
Seeds of thought take flight and roam,
Hoping to find a fertile home.

With each breeze, intentions rise,
Painting dreams across the skies.
Like a compass, winds will steer,
Guiding hearts to what is clear.

In the quiet, motives bloom,
Chasing light, dispelling gloom.
Every breath a chance to change,
Life's vast canvas, bold, and strange.

As the storms may come to play,
Winds of intention show the way.
Firmly rooted, we will stand,
With open hearts, united hand.

In the stillness, trust the flow,
Let the winds of spirit grow.
For in flight, our hopes align,
With each gust, our lives entwine.

Poetic Revelations

In the ink, secrets unfold,
Lines of passion, tales retold.
Every verse a world anew,
Painting thoughts in shades of blue.

With each stanza's tender grace,
We find shelter in this space.
Words awaken, feelings true,
Revelations, bright and few.

From the heart, the pen takes flight,
Dancing softly in the night.
In the rhythm, dreams emerge,
Through the lines, our souls converge.

In the silence, wisdom flows,
Guiding hearts where love bestows.
Every whisper, sweet release,
In these verses, find your peace.

As the pages turn and sway,
Poetic truths will light our way.
In this journey, hand in hand,
With each poem, together stand.

Tremors of the Spirit

In shadows deep, the whispers rise,
A tremor shakes the quiet skies.
Unseen forces, softly tread,
Awakening dreams long thought dead.

Through the valleys, echoes roam,
Carrying tales of a distant home.
Hearts aglow with flickering light,
Guided gently through the night.

In every crack, in every seam,
The spirit stirs, igniting dream.
A dance of hope, a fleeting chance,
Calling forth a timeless dance.

The mountains rise, the rivers flow,
In unity, the spirits grow.
Tremors shift the ground we stand,
Binding us with silent hand.

Essence of the Intangible

In the air, a quiet sigh,
Moments drift, like clouds on high.
Colors fade, yet feelings bloom,
In the stillness, life finds room.

Threads of thought, spun with care,
Bind the heart to what is rare.
Through the mist, we find our way,
Essence whispers, here to stay.

Emotions dance, yet can't be seen,
Crafting worlds where we have been.
Truth in silence, deep and wide,
Inbetween, we choose to bide.

Dreams alight on wings of grace,
In the intangible, we find space.
Breath of life, in twilight's glow,
In every heartbeat, love will flow.

Chime of True Selves

Across the fields, a gentle ring,
Voices chime, the spirits sing.
In every heart, a tale unfolds,
A melody of truths retold.

Cascading notes, a vibrant tide,
In harmony, we find our guide.
Stripped of masks, we stand revealed,
Chiming hearts, a force concealed.

With every pulse, the echoes rise,
A chorus born of angry skies.
Through the noise, a song is found,
In true selves, we are unbound.

Resonance deep within our core,
Chiming spirits, evermore.
As one we stand, in light's embrace,
Finding joy in shared grace.

Underground Harmonies

Beneath the surface, roots entwine,
Silent whispers in the pine.
In the soil, secrets keep,
Ancient echoes, buried deep.

Through the dark, the melodies flow,
Hidden rhythms, softly grow.
Voices rise from depths below,
In harmony, the earth will glow.

Glimmers twine where shadows play,
In the underground, they find their way.
Life unearths what lies concealed,
With each note, the heart is healed.

Resonant tones in twilight hum,
From the roots, the song is spun.
Together strong, with every breath,
An embrace that conquers death.

Curved Paths of Emotion

In shadows cast by fading light,
Whispers linger through the night.
A journey twirls, a gentle sway,
As feelings bloom, then slip away.

Each heartbeat dances, soft, sincere,
Mapping secrets that we hold dear.
With every turn, a story spun,
In curved paths where our dreams run.

Through winding roads, we laugh and cry,
As memories flutter, like birds flying high.
Beneath the stars, we find our way,
In the tender moments where we stay.

The echoes of laughter, the sighs of pain,
Flow like rivers through joy and rain.
In embrace of sorrow, joy is found,
On this emotional battleground.

So let us wander, hand in hand,
In this rich, uncharted land.
With each step, we learn and grow,
In curves of emotion, deep and slow.

Waves of Sentiment

Upon the shore, the tides will rise,
Carrying dreams across the skies.
Each wave a whisper, soft and sweet,
Crashing gently at our feet.

Sentiments swirl like leaves in flight,
Painting portraits in morning light.
With every crest, a memory found,
In the ocean's heartbeat, love unbound.

The ebb and flow, a timeless dance,
Each swell invites a second chance.
Through calm and storm, our spirits sail,
As tides of feeling never fail.

Beneath the surface, secrets hide,
In currents only we abide.
With open hearts and open minds,
In waves of sentiment, peace entwined.

Together we'll surf these emotional seas,
Riding high on hope's gentle breeze.
For when we're lost, we'll find our way,
In the waves that carry us each day.

Chasing Fleeting Moments

In the dance of time, we chase the light,
Moments flicker, shining bright.
Like fireflies in a summer's eve,
They rise and fall, we dare believe.

Each breath counts down the clock's embrace,
As laughter echoes in this space.
We grasp at shadows, soft and fair,
Only to find they linger rare.

Through tangled paths, we run so fast,
In pursuit of treasures that seldom last.
Eyes wide open, we seek to find,
The fleeting whispers of the mind.

With every heartbeat, a chance to seize,
Every glance holding memories like leaves.
We tread the line 'twixt here and gone,
In chasing moments just like dawn.

So let us rise, with spirit bold,
Embracing stories yet untold.
In fleeting moments, love will bloom,
In cherished echoes, we dispel the gloom.

Heartfelt Labyrinths

In winding halls of dreams we tread,
Through heartfelt mazes, hope is led.
Each corner turned, a thrill awaits,
In this labyrinth where love creates.

With vibrant hues that softly blend,
We seek the paths that never end.
Through echoes of laughter, whispers soar,
Each step, a promise, forevermore.

In tangled vines of time and grace,
We lose ourselves in this embrace.
Finding solace in the unknown,
In heartfelt labyrinths, we're never alone.

Together we wander, hand in hand,
Within these twists, our hearts understand.
In shadows deep, our spirits meet,
In every challenge, love's defeat.

So let the journey be our guide,
As we traverse this endless ride.
In this labyrinth, we'll find our way,
With heartfelt whispers that forever stay.

Mapping the Inner Landscape

In the stillness, shadows play,
Winding paths where thoughts can stray.
Fleeting glimpses of the soul,
Charting dreams, they make us whole.

Mountains rise where fears may dwell,
Hidden valleys, truths to tell.
In the depths, a river flows,
Carving edges, beauty grows.

Each moment a compass guide,
With courage, we will not hide.
Stars above, they light the night,
Guiding hearts with gentle light.

Winds of change whisper and hum,
Echoes of a beating drum.
Finding paths both new and old,
In this map, our stories told.

Fleeting Yet Eternal

Time dances on a fragile thread,
Moments pass, yet linger ahead.
In the blink, a memory shines,
A fleeting glance, where love aligns.

Petals fall, yet seeds remain,
In quiet echoes, joy and pain.
Every heartbeat, a timeless chance,
In the void, we learn to dance.

Waves of change, a gentle tide,
Whispered wishes, dreams collide.
In the chaos, beauty swells,
Fleeting tales that time compels.

Hold the fleeting, treasure the now,
In the eternal, we take a bow.
Each breath a story, written clear,
Moments cherished, always near.

Sose of the Heart's Whisper

In a hush, the heart will speak,
Softest echoes, tender, meek.
Like a breeze that stirs the trees,
Whispers of love float on the seas.

Glimmers shine in silent night,
Words unspoken, dreams take flight.
In the shadows, secrets twirl,
In the silence, emotions swirl.

Every sigh, a tale unfolds,
In the gentle dark, life molds.
Stripped of noise, the truth comes clear,
In the stillness, we draw near.

Listen close, for wisdom lies,
In the pauses, life replies.
Hearts entwined, in quiet grace,
Finding solace, our sacred space.

Unspoken Canvases

Blank pages wait for colors bright,
Lines unwritten, pure and light.
With a brush, our dreams ignite,
Each stroke a vision, taking flight.

Silent canvases, hearts display,
The hues of life, in rich array.
Shadows dance, the light will blend,
In the art, beginnings end.

Palette rich with tales untold,
Every whisper, soft and bold.
In the spaces, stories live,
In silence, we learn to give.

Every heartbeat, a new design,
In unspoken realms, we align.
Crafting moments, brush and hand,
On unspoken canvases, we stand.

Frequencies of Love

In the silence, hearts collide,
Whispers dance, side by side.
Melodies weave through the air,
Uniting souls with gentle flair.

In every glance, a spark ignites,
A rhythm found in starry nights.
Resonating through the deep,
Awakening dreams from sleep.

The pulse of joy runs clear and bright,
Guiding lost paths to the light.
A chorus sung, a sweet release,
In love's embrace, we find our peace.

In moments still, emotions flare,
Like autumn leaves that twist in air.
Underneath a world so vast,
Love's frequencies always last.

Echoes linger, soft and warm,
In every touch, there is a charm.
Through time, the waves will gently flow,
On this journey, love will grow.

Imprints on the Soul

Footsteps leave a mark so deep,
Memories shared, secrets we keep.
In the shadows of the past,
Our stories written, forever cast.

Tender glances, silent sighs,
As the moonlight fills the skies.
Each moment carved in heart and mind,
Binding us in love refined.

The warmth of laughter, sweet and rare,
Imprints of joy linger in the air.
Like the tide that ebbs and flows,
The soul remembers, ever knows.

In quiet hours, reflections arise,
Revealing truths behind our eyes.
The art of love—that timeless role,
Leaves eternal imprints on the soul.

With every heartbeat, stories unfold,
A tapestry of warmth and bold.
Together we write, together we dream,
Life's essence, a shimmering stream.

Velvet Echoes

In a world of whispered sighs,
Velvet echoes never die.
Softly spoken, hearts respond,
In the twilight, love's beyond.

Gentle touches, dreams align,
In secret corners, souls entwine.
Every heartbeat sings a song,
A vibrant tale where we belong.

The air is thick with memories,
Dancing leaves on autumn trees.
In the shadows, our secrets swell,
A universe where week can dwell.

Through the night, the heartbeat flows,
Caught in moments love bestows.
In the echoes, tender, sweet,
Our spirits meet, our lives complete.

With every laugh, with every tear,
Velvet echoes always near.
Together weaving, soft and bold,
Timeless stories waiting to be told.

Shadows of Affection

In the dusk, where shadows play,
Whispers linger, softly sway.
Affection paints the night aglow,
A warm embrace, a gentle flow.

Beneath the stars, love's tender gaze,
Guides us through the evening's haze.
With every pulse, it gently sighs,
Creating worlds beneath the skies.

In hidden paths, our hearts unite,
Dancing under the soft moonlight.
Each embrace, a promise shared,
In shadows thick, we are ensnared.

Through moments fleeting, time stands still,
In every glance, a sweet thrill.
With shadows drawn, we find our way,
In the depths where affections sway.

As dawn unfolds, we hold it tight,
Memories etched in morning light.
In the tapestry life does weave,
Shadows of affection, we believe.

Rhythms of the Inner Self

In whispers deep, the heart does sing,
A gentle pulse, a secret thing.
Each beat a truth, each pause a space,
Reflecting dreams, a tranquil grace.

Waves crash softly on the shore,
In solitude, we crave for more.
Echoes of self in silence found,
In stillness, our spirits unbound.

Through shadows cast by fears we face,
Emerges light, a warm embrace.
The rhythms dance, a sacred rite,
Leading us toward the light.

Threads of joy, of sorrow spun,
In every beat, we become one.
Mind and soul in harmony,
Embracing what it means to be.

Beneath the layers, truths unveil,
In every heart, the stories trail.
A journey mapped in silent tones,
The inner self finds its own home.

Secrets in Soft Breaths

Beneath the sky, beneath the stars,
Whispers linger, soft as ours.
In each breath, a tale untold,
Inhaled mysteries, precious gold.

When twilight falls, and shadows creep,
The secrets wait, in dreams they sleep.
A tender touch on weary skin,
Inhaling peace, we breathe within.

Gentle moments linger still,
Nature's sound, an ancient thrill.
Fleeting hopes like wind may fade,
Yet in soft breaths, love is made.

On quiet nights when hearts align,
Unspoken words, a sacred sign.
In hushed tones, we find our way,
As secrets bloom at break of day.

With every sigh, we release fears,
A symphony of unspilled tears.
In soft breaths, a life reborn,
When dawn breaks, we welcome morn.

Cadence of Yearning

In the stillness of the moonlight glow,
Whispers of longing begin to flow.
Each heart beat, a soft refrain,
Yearning echoes, joy and pain.

Caught in dreams that drift and sway,
Silent wishes that fade away.
The pulse of hope, a gentle nudge,
Awakens feelings that won't budge.

Distance calls, a lover's song,
Reminds us where we all belong.
The ache of wanting, deep and true,
In every shadow, I seek you.

Moments linger, sweet as wine,
A dance of souls, yours and mine.
Cadence builds, each note a spark,
In yearning hearts, ignites the dark.

As starlit skies hold secret dreams,
In every breath, the memory gleams.
Though time may weave its tangled thread,
The cadence of yearning will be fed.

Symphony of Tenderness

In every glance, a story shared,
A symphony where hearts are bared.
Note by note, the music plays,
In tranquil moments, love displays.

Each whisper soft, like silk on skin,
Opens doors we once hid within.
Tender gestures, gentle and true,
In quiet spaces, I find you.

The laughter blends with sighs of bliss,
In every heartbeat, a tender kiss.
Together we weave, a tapestry bright,
A symphony born in soft twilight.

The rhythm sways, both calm and wild,
In shadows dance, we're love's own child.
With every note, we redefine,
In kindness shared, our souls entwine.

Through every storm, and gentle breeze,
Tenderness brings us to our knees.
In this embrace, we find our song,
A symphony of love so strong.

Intonations of Belief

In the silence, whispers call,
Faith flickers, a gentle thrall.
Hearts unite in quiet grace,
A shared smile, the sacred space.

Echoes rise on hopeful winds,
Through the doubt, the spirit spins.
Promises in the starlit night,
Guiding souls with radiant light.

In the shadows, courage grows,
Each step forward, belief bestows.
Hands held tight, together we stand,
The pulse of hope, a promised land.

Each journey starts with a dream,
Through the dark, we gleam and beam.
Voices blend in a soothing song,
A tapestry where all belong.

With each heartbeat, faith reborn,
In the light of a hopeful morn.
Weaving trust in every verse,
A universe we will traverse.

Silhouettes of Sentiment

In the twilight, shadows dance,
Silhouettes in a wistful trance.
Memories fade but linger still,
Captured whispers, hearts to fill.

Beneath the stars, dreams take flight,
Tender moments, pure delight.
Glimmers of love in every sigh,
Holding hope as days pass by.

In laughter's echo, joy we find,
Tangled thoughts with hearts entwined.
Through the storms and calm, we glide,
Together, there's nothing to hide.

With every stroke, a tale we weave,
In colors bright, we learn to believe.
Softened edges of pain and bliss,
In shadows cast, a gentle kiss.

In the dawn's embrace, feelings wake,
Silhouettes shift, a new path to take.
Hand in hand, we traverse the night,
Crafting dreams in the morning light.

Harmonies of Humanity

In the heart of every face,
Lives a story, lives a grace.
Voices blend, a chorus wide,
Together we rise, side by side.

A melody of hope we sing,
In the silence, joy takes wing.
Kindred spirits, hands interlace,
Creating beauty in this space.

Through the trials, we unite,
Holding on to what is right.
With each note, a bond is made,
Breaking barriers, unafraid.

In the laughter, in the tears,
We find solace through the years.
A symphony of love and grace,
Humanity's warm, sweet embrace.

As the world spins, we stand tall,
In the harmony, we hear the call.
A choir of souls, forever free,
Singing songs of unity.

Trill of Transcendence

In the stillness, echoes flow,
A whisper of the world we know.
With each heartbeat, rise and glide,
Transcendence waits, we cannot hide.

On the breeze, sacred notes sway,
Guiding hearts to light the way.
In twilight's glow, a spark ignites,
Reaching for those starry heights.

In the silence, truths unfold,
Stories of the brave and bold.
With each trill, we rise anew,
Finding strength in the pure and true.

Through the shadows, hope shall soar,
Breaking chains forevermore.
In unity, we rise and bend,
Transcendence finds us, hand in hand.

Where the soul's song echoes bright,
In harmony, we chase the light.
Eternal beauty, we create,
In the trill, our hearts elate.

Refrains of the Unknown

Whispers echo through the night,
Shadows dance in fading light.
Secrets linger, softly tread,
Paths untaken, words unsaid.

Veils of mystery wrap the sky,
Stars like questions, drifting high.
Time stands still, a breath divine,
In the quiet, thoughts entwine.

Cascading dreams of what could be,
Floating gently, wild and free.
Fingers reach for distant shores,
Yet the heart's a locked-up door.

Each refrain, a haunting call,
In the silence, shadows stall.
Threads of fate begin to weave,
In the unknown, we believe.

Echoing through the vast expanse,
Life and mystery intertwine,
Lost in the web of night,
We seek the spark, the guiding light.

Hidden Beacons

In the depths of tangled woods,
Where only silence firmly broods,
Softly glows a distant flame,
Whispering the traveler's name.

Through the fog, a path is drawn,
Faintly lit by early dawn.
Footsteps follow, hearts aflame,
Knowing not just who to blame.

Crickets sing their midnight song,
While shadows stretch, both deep and long.
Secret truths lie intertwined,
In gentle whispers, fate aligned.

Veils are lifted, sights reveal,
Hidden beacons that can heal.
Guiding spirits, side by side,
To the light where dreams abide.

Embers flicker, softly bright,
In the dark, they share their light.
Find the courage, step forth free,
Hidden beacons lead to we.

Mosaic of Emotion

Colors blend in fractured light,
Emotions flutter, take their flight.
Each fragment tells a tale anew,
In the silence, feelings brew.

Textures woven through the threads,
Laughter mingles where hope spreads.
Joy and sorrow, hand in hand,
Rise like waves upon the sand.

Moments captured, softly held,
Stories whispered, hearts compelled.
A canvas painted wild and wide,
Each emotion, a song inside.

Crimson teardrops, golden cheer,
Every shade, a cherished year.
Fleeting glimpses, bold and brave,
In the mosaic, love will save.

Textures shift, the heart ignites,
In the dance of days and nights.
Lost in layers, we find peace,
Mosaic of emotion, never cease.

Silent Resonance

In the stillness, echoes bloom,
Whispers chase away the gloom.
Thoughts like ripples in the air,
Silent notes of self-aware.

Time drifts gently, soft and slow,
In this space, such truths will flow.
Hearts converse without a sound,
In this silence, love is found.

Melodies of quiet grace,
Lingering in this sacred space.
Thoughts entwined like vines of gold,
Stories woven, lives retold.

Underneath the moon's embrace,
We discover our true place.
In the silence, fears release,
Resonating, we find peace.

Harmony in whispers shared,
In the void, we are prepared.
For the beauty that we find,
Silent resonance, hearts aligned.

Lament of Lost Yearnings

In the shadows where dreams lie,
Echoes of promises drift by.
Soft whispers fade in the night,
Silent tears mask the lost light.

Once bright hopes now dim and weak,
Memories tangled, fragile and meek.
A heart in longing sings alone,
Yearning for love it has not known.

Time's cruel passage leaves its mark,
Fading embers spark the dark.
Promises whispered on the breeze,
Fleeting moments, lost with ease.

In the garden of what could be,
Blooms of sorrow, petals of glee.
Yet within the silence, a spark,
A whisper, a flame in the dark.

So I gather the shards of dreams,
Piecing together the silent screams.
With hope that someday I'll find way,
To mend what was broken and fray.

Symphony of Inner Whispers

Beneath the surface, thoughts collide,
Melodies echo, secrets confide.
A symphony plays in muted tones,
Rhythms of heart, sung in alone.

In the quiet, shadows dance free,
Whispers of dreams that no one can see.
Notes of desire float in the air,
A fragile tune, tender and rare.

Fingers trace paths of unseen sound,
Harmonies lost, yet always around.
Every silence speaks, softly it calls,
In the depths of the mind, where time stalls.

So listen closely, let melodies ring,
Every whisper a promise to bring.
In the orchestra of the soul's deep
A symphony waits, yearning to keep.

With every breath, the music flows,
Awakening life in the stillness, it grows.
In the heart's chamber, let it ignite,
A symphony born under the night.

Chorus of the Lost

In the forest where shadows loom,
Echoes wander through the gloom.
Each lost soul, a song to sing,
Together they dance, a ghostly ring.

Gentle whispers drift like fog,
Stories linger, memories clog.
In the silence, feel the pain,
Chorus of the lost, a haunting refrain.

Voices call from distant shores,
Dreams long faded behind closed doors.
Each heartbeat sings of what's been gone,
A melancholic melody, forlorn.

Yet within the grief, a thread remains,
Stitching joy in the unseen pains.
Together they blend, a tapestry vast,
An echo of futures shaped by the past.

So gather the songs of those unseen,
In the chorus of the lost, find what's been.
For every note holds a truth inside,
In harmony, the shattered souls abide.

Underneath the Stillness

Beneath the quiet, life does hum,
Under the surface, echoes come.
A heart beats softly, secrets dwell,
In the stillness, whispers tell.

The world rests lightly in its breath,
Veiled in calm, dancing with death.
Yet beneath, chaos finds its path,
A current flows, igniting the wrath.

In each heartbeat, a story waits,
Silent hopes at the universe's gates.
What lies hidden in twilight's embrace,
A dance of shadows, a timeless chase.

Listen closely, the stillness speaks,
A symphony dwells, no words it seeks.
In the silence lives a tale anew,
Underneath the stillness, find what's true.

Let the whispers guide you through night,
In stillness, discover the hidden light.
For underneath each quiet veil,
Lives a saga, a heartbeat's tale.

Whispers of the Soul

In the quiet night, dreams unfold,
Secrets of the heart, gently told.
Stars above, like eyes that see,
Whispers of the soul, setting free.

Echoes linger in the breeze,
Carrying thoughts, as hearts appease.
Moments fleeting, like shadows cast,
Memories linger, forever vast.

At the dawn, the light will break,
Awakening the dreams we make.
With each ray, a new hope sings,
Whispers dance on hopeful wings.

In the silence, truths arise,
Gentle murmur, no disguise.
Listen close, don't let it fade,
For in whispers, love is made.

As the dusk drapes shadows low,
In stillness, all emotions flow.
Trust the silence, embrace the whole,
In the whispers, find your soul.

Echoes of Emotion

In the chambers of the heart, they dwell,
Each echo holds a tale to tell.
Voices soft, yet deeply felt,
Emotions rise, the silence melts.

Laughter weaves through the air,
Joyful moments, beyond compare.
But sorrow's shadow, too, must play,
Echoes of emotion in disarray.

With the tide, feelings swell,
In the waves, there lies a spell.
Dancing gently, like leaves in flight,
Echoes shimmer in the light.

Longing whispers in the night,
Guided by a silver light.
Hope flickers like a flame,
In the echoes, we find our name.

As memories fade into the past,
The echoes of love forever last.
In the heart, a sacred space,
Where emotions find their grace.

Silent Serenade

In the stillness, a melody flows,
Notes of peace, where nature knows.
Gentle harmonies fill the air,
A silent serenade, soft and rare.

Beneath the stars, secrets are shared,
In quiet moments, souls are bared.
Songs of dusk dance with the night,
In the silence, hearts take flight.

With every breath, a pulse of sound,
In the hush, magic can be found.
Words unspoken, yet understood,
A silent serenade feels so good.

In nature's cradle, softly sway,
Whispers echo where shadows play.
The serenade of life unfolds,
In silent tales, the heart beholds.

Through every note, the heart will yearn,
In silent serenades, love returns.
Listen closely, be aware,
For beauty lives in silence rare.

Murmurs Beneath the Surface

In the depths, where feelings hide,
Murmurs brew, like a restless tide.
Subtle signs, calling softly near,
Beneath the surface, whispers clear.

Waves of thought crash and recede,
In hidden corners, hearts take heed.
Underneath the calm, tension brews,
Murmurs flow with unseen clues.

Gentle ripples against the stone,
In the silence, truths are known.
Listen past the noise and clamor,
For beneath lies the heart's true glamour.

As shadows deepen, feelings roam,
Murmurs guide us back to home.
Unspoken paths that softly wind,
Beneath the surface, love you'll find.

With every heartbeat, something stirs,
In whispered tones, life concurs.
Trust the murmurs, let them rise,
For in their depth, the soul complies.

Sorrows Yet to Sing

In shadows deep where silence dwells,
A tale of woe my spirit tells.
The weight of dreams, a heavy chain,
Each tear reflects a hidden pain.

Yet in the night, a spark will glow,
A whispered hope in softest flow.
Through darkest paths, I find the light,
A melody that breaks the night.

So sorrow sings in tender tones,
In quiet realms where comfort roams.
Each note a step, a gentle song,
To weave the heart where I belong.

With every loss, a lesson learned,
In embered hearts, the fire burns.
Through tangled webs of past regret,
I rise, I sing, I won't forget.

The echoes fade but still they stay,
A haunting tune that guides my way.
For in the pain, a truth will rise,
Amongst the tears, my spirit flies.

Palettes of Heartfelt Echoes

In colors bright, emotions swirl,
A canvas painted with every pearl.
Each stroke a whisper, soft and free,
Palettes of heart, your love for me.

From reds of passion to blues of calm,
Every shade a soothing balm.
The yellows spark like morning light,
In hues of joy, we take to flight.

In grays of doubt, we find our way,
With brush in hand, we dare to play.
The strokes may falter, but hearts remain,
Together we dance through joy and pain.

A portrait formed in laughter's glow,
Through trials faced, our colors grow.
In every hue, a story spun,
Of battles lost and victories won.

Yet still the echoes softly call,
In shades of love, we rise, never fall.
For what we paint can never fade,
In memories made, our dreams cascade.

Yearning in Stillness

In the quiet hour, dreams take flight,
Yearning whispers in the night.
A heart that aches, a silent plea,
In stillness found, I long to be.

The world outside, a distant hum,
Yet here I sit, my thoughts succumb.
To thoughts of you that softly cling,
In every breath, my heart does sing.

Through moments paused, the time stands still,
A fragile wish, a tender thrill.
Each heartbeat echoes, longing calls,
In shadows deep, my spirit sprawls.

And though the night may stretch so long,
In silence wrapped, I feel you strong.
A gentle touch from far away,
In stillness found, our souls will sway.

For every sigh, a prayer is cast,
A love that transcends, a bond so vast.
In every star, a spark of you,
My yearning heart finds peace anew.

Caress of the Cosmic

Starlight whispers in the dark,
Celestial dance ignites a spark.
Nebulas swirl in silent grace,
Infinity holds a warm embrace.

Galaxies weave a radiant song,
Echoes of ages where we belong.
Time drips softly through the night,
Guiding our hearts to the cosmic light.

Planets hum in their gentle spin,
Caressing dreams deep within.
Waves of wonder float and glide,
In the universe's arms, we abide.

Comets trail their shimmering tears,
Concealing hopes through countless years.
Each twinkle a promise we pursue,
In the vast cosmos, I find you.

The galaxies teach as they align,
Whispers of fate in every sign.
Let us wander where stars align,
In the caress of the cosmic divine.

Illuminated Heartstrings

In shadows deep, our spirits meet,
Threads of light intertwine, so sweet.
Echoing laughter, a tender tune,
Under the silver glow of the moon.

Every heartbeat plays a note,
With every whisper, our hearts float.
Bridges built from dreams and sighs,
Illuminated paths beneath the skies.

Each glance a spark, igniting fire,
Pulling our souls, lifting higher.
Resonance of love that won't depart,
Tugging softly on heartstrings' art.

In melodies where we belong,
Dancing together, forever strong.
A symphony etched in the night,
As stars drift softly, lending light.

United as one, we find our grace,
Illuminated in this sacred space.
Melodies linger, timeless and true,
Heartstrings resonating, me and you.

Euphony of Embrace

In the hush of the gentle dawn,
Whispers swirl before they're gone.
Softly cradled in morning's glow,
The euphony of love starts to flow.

Wrapped in warmth, we close our eyes,
Lost in a world where no one lies.
Each heartbeat sings a sweet refrain,
Embracing joy, dismissing pain.

Hands entwined in perfect grace,
Time stands still in this sacred place.
Together we dance, shadows merge,
In the euphony, our hearts surge.

With every sigh, the universe spins,
A celestial chord where love begins.
Harmony hums in tender space,
A melody spun from an eternal embrace.

In every note of whispered night,
Dreams illuminate our shared flight.
Euphony wrapped in softest lace,
Love, forever, in every embrace.

Hues of Hopefulness

As dawn breaks, colors unfurl,
Painting life in a vibrant swirl.
Each hue tells a story anew,
Whispers of dreams that will come true.

Soft pastels kiss the morning air,
Hopefulness lingers everywhere.
Every brushstroke, a promise holds,
In the canvas of life, dreams unfold.

Golden rays pierce through the gray,
Chasing shadows of yesterday.
In the laughter of children, we see,
The hues of hope painting you and me.

Crimson joy and sapphire tears,
Blend together through all our years.
Each moment a palette, wide and bright,
Crafting a tapestry filled with light.

In the twilight, colors ignite,
Filling our souls with pure delight.
Embracing the palette of our days,
In the hues of hopefulness, we gaze.

Harmony of True Feelings

In the shadow of the dawn,
Hearts rise like morning song,
Whispers dance on a breeze,
Tales of love that feel so strong.

In the stillness of the night,
Dreams weave through starlit skies,
Fingers touching gentle souls,
Where the silent truth lies.

Every heartbeat sings a tune,
Softly echoes through the air,
Playing notes of pure delight,
In a symphony we share.

In the garden of our hopes,
Petals fall, a fragrant blend,
Colors burst in warm embrace,
Nature's love that will not end.

Through the seasons we will dance,
With joy that knows no bounds,
In the harmony of true feelings,
Together, love resounds.

Notes from the Depths

Beneath the surface, secrets hide,
Whispers echo in the deep,
Dreams unfurl in the darkness,
Where desires silently creep.

Each moment a melody flows,
A tide pulling the heart's strings,
Lost in a symphony's depths,
Where hope and heartache sing.

The waves crash like crashing thoughts,
Submerged, yet still we yearn,
For the light that dances above,
And the lessons we must learn.

In the silence, voices rise,
Carving paths through the unknown,
Searching for glimpses of light,
In a world that feels alone.

From the depths, a song emerges,
Carried forth by hearts that dare,
Finding strength in shared stories,
In the love that lingers there.

Pulse of the Unheard

In the chaos of the day,
A pulse beats under the skin,
Words unspoken, yet they flow,
A tide that pulls us within.

Each rhythm tells a story,
Of dreams that dare to soar,
Silent hopes A whisper so loud,
That craves to be explored.

Through the hush of quiet hours,
Feels like time stands still,
A heartbeat racing softly,
With hopes that spark the will.

Echoes of what hasn't been,
Drift like shadows in the night,
Hearts that long for union,
To catch the moon's soft light.

The pulse continues, steady,
In every breath we take,
A song of dreams still waiting,
Awakening what's at stake.

Lyrical Longings

In every corner of the night,
A longing stirs the soul,
Notes drift softly through the air,
Filling spaces, making whole.

With each beat, a story speaks,
Of moments yet to see,
Dances twirling in the dark,
Where dreams can roam so free.

A constellation of desires,
Shimmering in endless grace,
Words written in the stars,
Guiding hearts to find their place.

In the symphony of silence,
We hear the world's sweet plea,
Longing for a touch of love,
In the harmony of we.

Through lyrical longings, we shall weave,
A tapestry of hope and light,
Together in this grand embrace,
In love's enduring flight.

Notes from the Depths

In shadows deep where whispers play,
The echoes hum of dreams lost gray,
Each sigh a tale of moments past,
In silence, memories are cast.

The tides of time, they ebb and flow,
With every heartbeat, secrets grow,
In the depths, where feelings dwell,
A treasure trove, each wish a spell.

From fathoms dark, a melody,
Resonates in harmony,
Each note a glimpse of what might be,
In depths below, we long to see.

With every breath, the darkness hums,
A symphony of pulse that drums,
In the quiet, life finds its way,
Through poignant tones of yesterday.

So listen close to the whispers near,
For in the dark, all becomes clear,
In the depths where dreams entwine,
The heart's own song, a truth divine.

Chants of the Boundless

Beyond the hills where eagles soar,
The spirit sings forevermore,
In every gust, a timeless call,
To wander wide, to rise, to fall.

The sky unfolds in hues of blue,
A canvas bright, forever new,
In open air, we find our place,
With every chant, we touch the grace.

The stars above, they wink and shine,
In endless night, their dance divine,
Each twinkle tells a tale of hope,
In vast expanse, we learn to cope.

With winds that guide our soul's ascent,
In freedom's hymn, we find content,
The boundless realm invites our hearts,
To sing aloud, to play our parts.

So join the call, let voices rise,
In unity beneath the skies,
For in each chant, the world awakes,
With every sound, a dream remakes.

Beats of Belonging

In rhythmic pulse, our hearts unite,
A bond unbroken, pure delight,
Through every beat, a story flows,
In this embrace, our spirit grows.

Each footstep echoes on the ground,
In every laugh, a love profound,
The tie that binds, both strong and true,
In shared moments, we start anew.

With gentle hands, we hold the night,
In glowing warmth, our souls take flight,
The melody of life we weave,
In every note, we dare believe.

Through trials faced and triumphs won,
In every heartbeat, we're as one,
The tapestry of life unfolds,
With threads of warmth and tales retold.

So keep the beat, let spirits soar,
In harmony, we seek for more,
For in this dance, we all belong,
A symphony, forever strong.

Waves of Sentiment

On shores of thought, the waters rise,
In gentle swells, the heart replies,
Each wave a whisper of the past,
In tides of feeling, deep and vast.

The ocean breathes, a lullaby,
With every crest, we laugh and sigh,
In every crash, a story shared,
In salty air, our souls declared.

The ebb and flow, a constant dance,
In each retreat, we find our chance,
To dive within, embrace the pain,
In watery depths, love's sweet refrain.

With every rise, new dreams emerge,
In waves of hope, our spirits surge,
Connected by the vast unknown,
In currents deep, we've always grown.

So let the sea caress your heart,
In waves of sentiment, never part,
For in the tide, we find our way,
With every surge, a brand new day.

Chords of Connection

In the melody of shared dreams,
Hearts find their perfect tune.
Fingers brush the strings of fate,
Creating rhythms under the moon.

With every note, a bond is formed,
Echoes of laughter fill the air.
Together we rise, unbreakable,
A symphony beyond compare.

In quiet moments, we still play,
The chords of love, a gentle sway.
Resonating through the night,
Guiding us with their soft light.

Miles may stretch, yet we remain,
Connected by the songs we sing.
In the chorus of our lives,
Joy and hope begin to spring.

So let the music flow and soar,
A testament to what we share.
In the chords of connection,
Together, nothing can compare.

Cadence of Compassion

In the softness of a gentle tear,
Lies the strength of empathy.
With open hearts, we draw near,
In the cadence of compassion, we are free.

Through trials faced and burdens shared,
A symphony of kindness grows.
With whispered words, our love declared,
In every act, compassion flows.

Together we rise, hand in hand,
Navigating the storms of life.
In unity, we take our stand,
Turning sorrow into light.

With every touch, the world feels whole,
A rhythm that binds us tight.
In the cadence of compassion,
We find solace deep in the night.

Let our hearts beat in sync,
Creating waves of gentle grace.
In this dance, we shall link,
Compassion's warmth, our shared embrace.

Feelings Woven in Starlight

In the night sky, our dreams ignite,
Whispers of wishes take their flight.
With every twinkle, hearts align,
Feelings woven in starlight, divine.

The cosmos paints our tales above,
In constellations, we find love.
Guided by stars, we'll explore,
Mapping emotions we can't ignore.

Each pulse of light, a story told,
Moments cherished, treasures bold.
Under the vast celestial sea,
We discover who we're meant to be.

As the night wraps us in its glow,
Silent promises softly flow.
With hearts aglow and spirits bright,
We dance together in the night.

So let us dream beneath the skies,
Feelings woven, never shy.
In the tapestry of the stars,
Our love, forever, truly ours.

Whispers on the Wind

A soft breeze carries your name,
Through leaves and trees, it weaves a game.
In every rustle, a secret sways,
Whispers on the wind, through endless days.

Like petals drifting through the air,
Your laughter lingers everywhere.
Each gust a memory, sweet and kind,
Connecting our souls, forever entwined.

With every sigh, the world stands still,
Emotions rise, a gentle thrill.
The whispers tell of love's embrace,
In harmony, we find our place.

Through valleys low and mountains high,
The winds carry our dreams to the sky.
Bound by the breath of nature's call,
In the whispers, we discover all.

So listen closely, let it be known,
In every whisper, love has grown.
With open hearts, we start to see,
The magic of whispers, you and me.

Verses of Vulnerability

In shadows deep, we hide our fears,
Whispers soft that only pain hears.
A fragile heart, it seeks to mend,
In silence held, it dares to bend.

Each tear that falls, a silent cry,
For strength in weakness, we question why.
Through cracks of light, hope starts to peek,
In embracing truth, we learn to speak.

A hand extended, not far to reach,
In shared understanding, love can teach.
With every story, a bond is formed,
In vulnerability, hearts are warmed.

The weight we carry, it may seem grand,
Yet here together, we take a stand.
In simple trust, we find our song,
In being real, we learn we're strong.

So let us weave a tapestry,
Of open hearts, a unity.
In this embrace, we shed our guise,
And in our truth, we'll find our rise.

Chant of the Spirit

In the stillness, a gentle call,
A melody that binds us all.
Through valleys low and mountains high,
The spirit sings beneath the sky.

With every breath, we find our pulse,
A rhythm pure, a cosmic waltz.
In nature's arms, we learn to flow,
The chant of life begins to grow.

From whispered winds to rustling leaves,
The essence of the world believes.
In unity, we dance and sway,
In spirit's light, we find our way.

With eyes closed tight, we hear the sound,
Of ancient truths that wrap around.
Each heartbeat is a sacred sign,
A connection, vast and divine.

We rise as one, hands intertwined,
In every soul, an echo twined.
Together strong, we lift our voice,
In harmony, we'll always rejoice.

Pulses of Passion

In fiery hearts where dreams ignite,
Desire dances, wild and bright.
With every glance, the world turns fast,
In moments fleeting, shadows cast.

A breath of air, electric thrill,
With courage found, we chase the fill.
In whispered words, our secrets share,
In passion's grip, we lay us bare.

Through storms we ride, the tides may change,
Yet in our hearts, we feel the range.
A flame once sparked, it cannot die,
In every longing, we learn to fly.

The pulses quicken, bass and drum,
In love's embrace, we find our home.
With every heartbeat, every beat,
In passion's dance, we feel complete.

So let us plunge into the fire,
With every step, a shared desire.
In the depths of all we chase,
Together we create our space.

Unraveled Emotions

Threads of feelings, tightly wound,
In every corner, truth is found.
To unravel fears, let silence speak,
In chaos soft, we find the weak.

A tear-streaked face, a heart exposed,
In vulnerability, life's composed.
With gentle hands, we weave the fray,
In messy love, we find our way.

With every heartbeat, stories flow,
In layers peeled, we come to know.
The weight of joy, the depth of sorrow,
In each emotion, we craft tomorrow.

Let us not shy from the raw and real,
In sacred spaces, together we heal.
For in our truths, we find belief,
In shared existence, we gather relief.

So breathe it in and let it out,
In every moment, live without doubt.
For in the unraveling, we see the light,
In the tapestry of life, we unite.

Songs of the Unseen

Whispers dance through silent air,
Soundless echoes, secrets share.
Beneath the veil, truth takes flight,
In shadows deep, we find our light.

Forgotten dreams in twilight glow,
Where whispers linger, rivers flow.
Unseen threads of fate entwine,
Binding hearts in the divine.

In gentle sighs, we hear the call,
The world's heartbeat, a soulful thrall.
Each note a promise, faint yet clear,
In the unseen, love draws near.

The tapestry of night unfolds,
With every story, life beholds.
Songs of starlight, soft and free,
In darkness, we find harmony.

So let the silence be our guide,
As unseen forces love abide.
In every heartbeat, every breath,
We sing our songs beyond all death.

Intimacy in the Shadows

In twilight hours, our secrets blend,
Silent gestures, emotions send.
Underneath the veil of night,
Two souls meet in tender light.

Whispers linger, soft and low,
Hidden truths in the afterglow.
Moments shared in quiet grace,
A stolen glance, a warm embrace.

In shadows cast by candlelight,
We find warmth, banishing fright.
With every touch, our hearts align,
Intimacy, a sacred sign.

Outside the world, a distant rush,
In here, only the gentle hush.
With every breath, we draw in close,
This quietude we value most.

As night unfolds, our fears subside,
In shadows, love becomes our guide.
A dance unspoken, yet so bold,
In intimacy, our hearts unfold.

Lullaby of the Unspoken

Softly spoken, words unyield,
In silence, dreams are revealed.
Under stars, our wishes flow,
In whispered hopes, we seem to grow.

Nighttime cradles every sigh,
As lullabies in silence lie.
Between the lines of what we knew,
The heart's language sings so true.

With every heartbeat, soft and slow,
A lullaby, life's gentle glow.
In tender moments, shadows blend,
Unspoken love, a timeless trend.

As moonlight casts its silver sheen,
We find solace in the serene.
Beneath the quiet, dreams awake,
A whispered promise we shall make.

In lullabies of the night,
Our souls dance in pure delight.
Together, in this gentle space,
Unspoken love, our warm embrace.

Harmonies of Hope

In darkest hours, a spark ignites,
Harmonies soar, chasing the night.
Through every storm, a song takes flight,
Whispers of hope in the pale moonlight.

With every note, a promise thrives,
In melodies, the spirit thrives.
Together we rise, hand in hand,
Building dreams on sunlit sand.

As rainbows greet after the rain,
We find strength in shared refrain.
Voices united, hearts entwined,
In harmonies, we seek and find.

Through trials deep, we still believe,
In every moment, we achieve.
With hope as our guiding star,
We'll journey on, no matter how far.

So let the music fill the air,
A symphony of love and care.
In every heartbeat, every scope,
Together we sing our harmonies of hope.

Essence of Euphoria

In the light of dawn, we rise,
Chasing dreams that fill the skies.
With laughter soft as morning dew,
The world awakens, fresh and new.

Hearts entwined in joy's embrace,
Every moment, a sweet chase.
With each breath, life dances free,
Euphoria in unity.

Colors swirl in vibrant hues,
Painting life with love we choose.
Whispers sweet, like summer breeze,
In our hearts, we find our ease.

Sparks ignite in evening's glow,
In twilight's bliss, our feelings flow.
Hand in hand, we face the night,
Together, our spirits ignite.

In the essence of our glee,
We find a long-lost melody.
With every beat, our souls align,
In this euphoric state, divine.

Murmurs of Memory

In shadows cast by time's embrace,
Whispers linger in this space.
Fleeting moments softly call,
Echoes dancing, rise and fall.

Old photographs of faded days,
Sunlit smiles and childhood plays.
Fragments of a life once lived,
In the silence, we're forgiven.

Each fleeting glance, a story told,
In the warmth of memories bold.
Time, a river, flows so fast,
Yet these whispers ever last.

Hearts remember what eyes forget,
In quiet corners, we still met.
With every sigh, a link remains,
Binding joys and all the pains.

As days dissolve into the night,
Memory's stars, our guiding light.
We hold these treasures, pure and true,
In every echo, me and you.

Sonnet of Sighs

In shadows deep, where hearts reside,
A gentle sigh, a silent guide.
Whispers weave through night's embrace,
In sighs, we find our hidden grace.

Each exhale sings a tale of love,
Soft as feathers from above.
In long-lost dreams and unspoken lies,
We linger still, in sonnets of sighs.

Time drifts slowly, yet it flies,
Caught between the truth and lies.
In every sob, sweet hope applies,
And in each heartbeat, life complies.

Through seasons changing, we hold tight,
In every breath, a spark ignites.
Together wrapped in twilight's guise,
Our souls shall dance in sonnets of sighs.

With every glance and fleeting touch,
We capture feelings that mean so much.
In the depth of night when love defies,
We pen our tales in sonnets of sighs.

Embraces in Silence

In quiet rooms, our hearts align,
Two souls entwined, a bond divine.
No words are needed, just a glance,
In the hush, we find romance.

The space between us, filled with peace,
In stillness, all our worries cease.
With gentle warmth, our spirits blend,
In silence deep, we find our friend.

A touch, a sigh, a knowing smile,
Together, we can pause awhile.
In every heartbeat, love's embrace,
In silence soft, we find our place.

Through whispered nights and endless days,
In stillness, we accept life's ways.
With arms that hold, our fears subside,
In silent love, we cannot hide.

So let the world around us fade,
In silent arms, our dreams are made.
Together here, in love's embrace,
In joyful silence, we find grace.

Dances of Devotion

In fields of gold where shadows lay,
Hearts entwined in a rhythmic sway,
Soft whispers float like petals in air,
Each movement speaks of love and care.

Beneath the moon, two spirits glide,
Glances exchanged, no need to hide,
With every turn, their souls align,
In this embrace, the stars define.

The melody of laughter rings,
In the closeness, sweetness clings,
Melting worries, freeing space,
In this moment, they find grace.

Through trials faced, their bond grows strong,
In every step, they right the wrong,
With tattered hearts, they learn to bloom,
In love's dance, they banish gloom.

So let them twirl under night's embrace,
For in this dance, they find their place,
With every leap and gentle sigh,
Devotion written in the sky.

Flickers of Affection

In the quiet corners, sparks ignite,
Soft glances shared, a fleeting light,
A tender brush, the warmth of skin,
In simple moments, affection begins.

Whispers exchanged in the fading day,
Each word a promise, here to stay,
Fading doubts with each gentle smile,
In every heartbeat, they linger awhile.

Memory dances in twilight's glow,
With laughter echoing, soft and low,
Fingers entwined like vines in bloom,
In this cocoon, they dispel the gloom.

Little gestures, soft as a dove,
Breathe in the essence of their love,
Flickers bright in this cozy embrace,
Each fleeting moment, their sacred space.

Through shadows long, their light will stay,
In flickers of affection, come what may,
For in each heartbeat, they come alive,
In every moment, their love will thrive.

Threads of Vulnerability

In the quiet depths, souls laid bare,
Threads of truth float in the air,
Each confession a delicate weave,
In vulnerability, they learn to believe.

With heavy hearts, they stitch and mend,
Bringing light where shadows bend,
Open arms in a world so wide,
In honest moments, they find pride.

Every secret shared, a sacred bond,
With trust as their shelter, a haven fond,
They unravel fears, expose the raw,
In threads of love, they find their flaw.

A fragile dance of give and take,
Holding space for each other's ache,
In this embrace, they learn to heal,
Fostering strength in the wounds they feel.

So let them entwine through joy and strife,
With threads of vulnerability, they find life,
In every tear and every smile,
They weave a tapestry, each thread worthwhile.

Tides of Thought

Upon the shore, thoughts flow like streams,
Waves of wonder, chasing dreams,
In silence, they rise, then softly fall,
Tides of thought, answering the call.

Days drift past in a gentle breeze,
Worries fade like footprints on seas,
Each wave a moment, crashing then still,
In the ebb and flow, they find their will.

Underneath the vast, starry sky,
Thoughts take flight, learning to fly,
With whispers of hope dancing anew,
Tides of thought, forever true.

For every current that sweeps along,
Brings lessons learned, both weak and strong,
In the ocean of mind, the spirit roams,
Finding solace in familiar homes.

So ride the tides where dreams collide,
In the depths of thought, there's no need to hide,
For in every wave that shapes the shore,
A universe whispers, forevermore.

Melodies Unseen

In whispers soft as evening's sigh,
The silent notes of dreams float high.
They dance like shadows, bright yet meek,
In every heart, they speak and peek.

The rustling leaves in twilight's glow,
Compose a tune the stars don't know.
Each heartbeat echoes with intent,
A lullaby of moments spent.

Unseen melodies weave through air,
A symphony of sweet despair.
They touch the soul, though eyes may close,
A tender warmth, where comfort grows.

With every breath, the music swells,
In quietude, the spirit dwells.
No words are needed, just the space,
Where harmonies and stillness chase.

As dawn arises, light breaks free,
The unseen songs, a legacy.
In every pulse, they find their flight,
Melodies unseen, in day and night.

Songs of the Inner Fire

Deep within, where passions roar,
A fire burns, forever more.
With every flicker, dreams take flight,
Illuminated by their light.

The heart ignites with fervent flame,
A call to rise, to stake a claim.
In every moment, courage flies,
As embers dance beneath the skies.

Awakened souls, we find our song,
In rhythm vast, where we belong.
Through trials faced and fears released,\nThe inner fire gives us peace.

A symphony of strength and grace,
Unfolds within this sacred space.
With every song, we rise and shine,
Embracing love, a bond divine.

Together we ignite the night,
With every heartbeat, pure delight.
In songs of old and vows we weave,
The inner fire, a gift we leave.

Rhythms of Desire

In twilight's glow, the pulse begins,
A dance of hearts, where silence spins.
The yearning deep, a timeless beat,
In shadows soft, our bodies meet.

With every glance, the rhythm sways,
In whispered words, the longing stays.
A cadence found in gentle touch,
The music flows; we crave so much.

Through tangled nights and fervent dreams,
The world fades out, or so it seems.
With every sigh, the tempo rises,
In passion's fire, truth disguises.

The heartbeat quickens, spirits fly,
In fierce embrace, we touch the sky.
Within this dance, we lose the light,
Desire's whispers, soft and bright.

In rhythms bold, we claim the night,
As souls unite, in pure delight.
With every pulse, the promise glows,
In timeless rapture, love bestows.

Resonance of the Unspoken

In silence wrapped, a truth resides,
The resonance where heart divides.
Words may falter, yet feelings soar,
In spaces deep, we ask for more.

The air is thick with what we feel,
A bond unbroken, raw and real.
Intentions woven without sound,
In quiet moments, hope is found.

With every glance that lingers long,
Our souls entwined in silent song.
The weight of dreams, unvoiced desires,
In fragile light, our hearts conspire.

In echoes soft, the shadows play,
Beyond the words we dare not say.
The resonance of vows unseen,
In every heartbeat, love's routine.

So let us tread on paths unknown,
In shared silence, we find our own.
In presence felt and plans unmade,
The unspoken love will never fade.

Cadence of Love

In whispers soft, two hearts entwine,
A dance of souls, a love divine.
With every beat, a rhythm true,
In silence speaks, the pulse of two.

Through twilight's glow, their shadows blend,
A symphony that knows no end.
In every glance, a story told,
A warmth that never fades or grows cold.

Beneath the stars, their dreams take flight,
The moonlit path, their guiding light.
With every laugh, the world retreats,
In love's embrace, their hearts complete.

In softest sighs, the echoes ring,
A melody only true hearts bring.
With hands held tight, they face the dawn,
In life's grand song, they're never gone.

Each whispered word, a gentle touch,
In every moment, they feel so much.
The cadence shifts, yet holds them near,
A timeless tune that draws them here.

Silent Serenades

Amidst the hush, a love unfolds,
In secret nights, the heart beholds.
With every glance, a whisper shared,
A silent song, two souls prepared.

In moonlit dreams, their spirits soar,
A quiet tune that asks for more.
With gentle sighs, they find their peace,
In tranquil moments, sweet release.

The stars align, a cosmic clue,
A melody both old and new.
Together bound, with hearts aglow,
In silent serenades, their love will grow.

In shadows deep, their laughter spills,
A soothing balm, a cure for ills.
With every heartbeat, they compose,
A symphony that never slows.

Through whispered nights, their dreams take flight,
A cherished bond, forever tight.
Within the silence, secrets blend,
In serenades that never end.

Intonation of Dreams

In twilight's glow, dreams softly call,
An intonation that binds us all.
With every hope, we craft our skies,
In colors bright, our spirits rise.

Through starlit paths, we wander free,
In dreams we find our true decree.
With whispered vows, we write our fate,
An intonation, never late.

In rustling leaves, we hear the song,
A melody where we belong.
With hands entwined, we chase the dawn,
In every beat, our dreams are drawn.

Each night we share, a canvas vast,
In strokes of light, our shadows cast.
With every tear, a story shared,
An intonation, deeply cared.

Through endless nights, we'll weave our thread,
In dreams we speak the words unsaid.
With every pause, our love will stream,
An intonation, pure and dream.

Melodic Secrets

In hidden places, whispers bloom,
A world of secrets, love's perfume.
With every touch, a note is played,
In rhythmic breaths, their hearts conveyed.

Through quiet rooms, their laughter spills,
A melody of joy that thrills.
With tender glances, stories weave,
In every moment, we believe.

Beneath the stars, they find their tune,
In melodic whispers, hearts attune.
With every sigh, a soft embrace,
In secret dreams, they find their place.

In shadowed corners, secrets thrive,
A dance of souls that feels alive.
With gentle words, the night extends,
In melodic secrets, love transcends.

Through every heartbeat, they'll align,
A song of love, forever fine.
With every note, their spirits soar,
In melodic secrets, they explore.

Beneath the Surface

In waters deep where shadows dwell,
Secrets hide, they weave a spell.
Ripples whisper, tales untold,
In silence, mysteries unfold.

Beneath the waves, a world unseen,
Echoes of what might have been.
Coral gardens, vibrant and bright,
Guardians of the moonlit night.

The silence speaks of ancient lore,
As tides return to kiss the shore.
Shells embrace the ocean's sigh,
Beneath the surface, dreams can lie.

With every splash, a heartbeat calls,
In liquid depths where freedom sprawls.
The gentle pull of ebb and flow,
A dance of life, a gentle show.

Discovering what's kept inside,
In silence, fear and hope collide.
Each drop a story, yet to weave,
In harmony, we dare believe.

Voices in the Quiet

In the hush where shadows creep,
Softly stir the thoughts we keep.
Whispers brush against the mind,
In solitude, the heart unwinds.

Each sigh a tale of dreams forlorn,
In silence, vibrant hopes are born.
Echoes linger, sharing light,
Painting colors in the night.

Stars above, they seem to know,
All the secrets down below.
In the quiet, fears do fade,
As solace in the stillness laid.

Voices rise like gentle streams,
Flowing softly through our dreams.
With every pause, we find a way,
To listen to what words don't say.

Embracing silence, hand in hand,
Understanding grows so grand.
In the stillness, hearts unite,
Voices echo in the night.

Symphony of the Unsaid

Beneath the words, the silence hums,
A cadence soft where stillness comes.
In every pause, a story waits,
Composed in whispers, love translates.

The notes of hope, they twist and turn,
In each unspoken, passions burn.
Harmony in muted tones,
Lingers where the heart atones.

A melody without a sound,
In gentle spaces, truths abound.
Every glance, a fleeting song,
The symphony where we belong.

With tender hearts, we dance alone,
In every silence, truth is shown.
A rhythm felt, a pulse sincere,
In quiet moments, love draws near.

The symphony, though oft unheard,
Is written deep, in every word.
In unexplained, emotions play,
In the quiet light of day.

Ballad of the Invisible

In shadows cast, they weave their threads,
With stories of the life they've led.
Invisible yet ever near,
In whispered winds, we sense their fear.

A fleeting glance, a gentle smile,
In silence strong, they walk awhile.
Each step unseen, yet deeply felt,
In hidden places, hearts can melt.

They linger close, in crowded space,
The unseen souls we can't embrace.
With every beat, their tales arise,
In ballads sung with unseen eyes.

Echoing through the timeless night,
A dance of shadows, bold and bright.
With hearts attuned, we hear the call,
Of those who rise beyond the fall.

In paths they tread, we find a way,
To honor those who long to stay.
The unseen bonds of love are strong,
In every silence, they belong.

Awakening of Affection

In the quiet dawn, hearts stir anew,
Whispers of feelings that gently break through.
Softly they bloom in the light of the morn,
A tapestry woven, where love is reborn.

Eyes meet in silence, an unspoken vow,
Leaves rustle softly, the world takes a bow.
Petals unfurl, in the warm sunny glow,
Two souls in harmony, a sweet ebb and flow.

Moments of laughter, a dance in the breeze,
Hearts entwined deeply, with effortless ease.
Time seems to pause, in that sacred embrace,
Awakening affection, a tender grace.

Stars in the twilight, their stories untold,
Promises linger, in glimmers of gold.
Hand in hand walking, through shadows of night,
Love's gentle spark, a most beautiful sight.

As dusk turns to dawn, and darkness to light,
Whispers of love, chase away every fright.
In the stillness, hear the heart's gentle call,
Awakening affection, encompassing all.

Crescendo of the Inward

In the still of the night, hear the silence hum,
Whispers of thoughts, like a distant drum.
Echoes of longing rise from deep within,
Inward we wander, where our truths begin.

Moments of stillness, a breath in the dark,
Flickering shadows, igniting a spark.
Through the corridors, where our spirits play,
We dance to the rhythms of the soul's ballet.

Thoughts flow like rivers, uncharted yet clear,
Carving our paths, as we draw ever near.
In the heart of the mind lies a symphony bright,
Crescendo of insight, emerging from night.

Questions linger softly, like stars in the sky,
Seeking the answers, yet daring to fly.
Each note a discovery, a story to tell,
Inwardly rising, as we weave our spell.

As dawn greets the silence, and dreams fade away,
The echoes of inward will forever stay.
A melody lingers, in the fabric of time,
Crescendo of the inward, a sublime rhyme.

Notes from the Spirit

From the depth of the heart, soft melodies play,
Whispers of wisdom in the light of the day.
Gentle reminders that urge us to soar,
Notes from the spirit, forever explore.

Each flicker of light brings a spark to ignite,
The beauty of living, through shadows and light.
Harmony dances in the breath of the trees,
Notes from the spirit, carried on the breeze.

In the still of the morning, the world comes alive,
Threads of connection, in which we all thrive.
Simple vibrations that guide us to see,
Notes from the spirit, setting us free.

As love intertwines with the fabric of fate,
Hands reach together, it's never too late.
Through laughter and sorrow, the spirits compose,
A symphony woven, where true solace grows.

With each rising sun, let the spirit prevail,
Embrace the journey, let the echoes sail.
For in every heartbeat, a sonnet will start,
Notes from the spirit, the song of the heart.

Lullabies of the Heart

In the cradle of night, where dreams softly weave,
Lullabies whisper, teaching us to believe.
Comforting rhythms, like rain on the ground,
Sweet lullabies cradle, where peace can be found.

Moonlight dances gently on faces aglow,
Stories of love in the soft, tender flow.
Each note like a feather, floats softly above,
Lullabies of the heart, wrapped in pure love.

Through the quiet moments, solace does bloom,
Harmony beckons from shadows and gloom.
A serenade echoes, through the still of the night,
Wrapping us closely in warmth and in light.

As stars twinkle softly, they join in the song,
A melody timeless, where all souls belong.
Embracing the stillness, where wishes unite,
Lullabies of the heart, a world dressed in light.

As dawn breaks anew, let the echoes arise,
Whispers of love beneath endless skies.
For each gentle lullaby, holds a promise so rare,
Lullabies of the heart, in the beauty we share.

Golden Threads of Connection

In the weave of life's design,
We find each other's hands,
Silken bonds that intertwine,
Stronger than we understand.

Through laughter shared and tears,
We stitch our stories tight,
Threads connecting heart and fears,
In day and quiet night.

Moments glimmer like the sun,
Woven in our DNA,
Every smile, every run,
Guides us through the fray.

Time has no edges or seams,
It flows like a gentle stream,
Together, we chase our dreams,
Bound by love's timeless beam.

In every glance, a spark,
Illuminating the dark,
In this tapestry, we learn,
Golden threads forever burn.

Words Beyond Words

Silent whispers fill the air,
In the hush, we find our way,
Messages we all can share,
In the heart's sweet ballet.

Eyes that speak, a soft embrace,
Knowing glances take their flight,
Every gesture finds its place,
In the rhythm of the light.

Language often falls away,
In a simple touch or sigh,
In the dance of night and day,
We communicate the why.

Stories written in the stars,
Soundless notes that grace the sky,
Boundless dreams behind our scars,
Sing the truth that words deny.

In the silence, love will bloom,
Words unspoken, pure and bright,
In the stillness, we consume,
The essence of pure delight.

Chasing the Elusive

Fleeting moments slip away,
Like shadows in the light,
We chase them, day by day,
Hoping to hold them tight.

Dreams dance on the edge of night,
Elusive as the stars,
Within our grasp, just out of sight,
Fading like old scars.

Life's briefest joys ignite,
In the fleeting game we play,
Holding dreams, a hopeful fight,
As they drift from light to gray.

Every heartbeat leads the way,
To treasures we can't find,
Yet still, we dance, come what may,
Keen to seek, to be unkind.

But in the chase, we find a spark,
A rhythm, pulse, a one-way street,
Though elusive, love leaves a mark,
In this dance, our souls meet.

Ripples of the Inner Sea

In the depths of mindful thought,
Waves of feelings start to rise,
Each emotion, tightly caught,
Beneath the sky's vast guise.

Ripples dance upon the shore,
Silent whispers touch the ground,
Echoes of what came before,
In the stillness, we are found.

Currents pull us to the core,
Where the soul's reflection lies,
Searching for what we adore,
In the sea, no need for guise.

Every wave tells a story,
Of love, loss, joy and pain,
In the depths, we find our glory,
In the sun and gentle rain.

Let the ripples guide our way,
Through the vast, mysterious sea,
In the journey, come what may,
We'll discover you and me.

Milton Keynes UK
Ingram Content Group UK Ltd.
UKHW022224251124
451566UK00006B/115